Copyright

The Big We
WE ARE ONE BIG FAMILY

© The Big We, We are one big family

Copyright © 2015 Sherilyn Bridget Avalon.

All rights reserved. No part of this book may be used or reproduced by any means, Graphic, electronic, or mechanical, including photocopying, recording, taping or by any Information storage retrieval system without the written permission of the publisher except in the case of brief quotations embodied in critical articles and reviews.

PLACE 33 PRESS, LLC

Books may be ordered through booksellers or by contacting:

 702-717-2137

Because of the dynamic nature of the Internet, any web addresses or links contained In this book may have changed since publication and may no longer be valid. The views expressed in this work are solely those of the author and do not necessarily reflects the views of the publisher, and the publisher hereby disclaim any responsibility for them.

Any people depicted in stock imagery provided by Think stock are models, and such images are being used for illustrative purposes only.

Author/ **Illustrator** / Sherilyn Bridget Avalon

ISBN: 978-0-9915700-7-2 (hc)

ISBN -ISBN: 978-0-9915700-5-8

Printed in the United States of America.

I dedicate this book to my family.

My awesome grandchildren, That I am blessed with.

Skyler, Trinity, Navarra, Lily, Braden, Jienna, and Zen.

They gave me my inspiration in writing and illustrating this book.

Love Grandma

The Big We

WHAT IS THE BIG WE?

The Big WE is what we are all part of...that part that connects us all at our heartstrings.

Let's say for example; you're passing by a house that is on fire, you hear someone crying out for help. You don't hesitate, you run toward the fire not thinking about the consequences till afterward. Because when you save that person, you are that person for a split second, you are essentially saving yourself.

The Spirit Within You

There is a Spirit within you, do you remember?

We are spiritual beings having a human experience.

We Are One Big Family!

We are all tied together as one, through our heart strings in this tapestry

called LIFE. What we do is felt through all of us, everyone in the whole world.

We must trust each other for the good of all.

Love Yourself More Today Than Yesterday!

Give to others from your heart, and see the love begin to start.

We are all connected. We are all energy...the trees, the rocks, the animals and you.

Thoughts Of Love Create Peace.

By the thoughts we create, we fill the world

with fresh ideas and solutions.

Grow Your Love Thoughts.

Think the thought = plant the seed.

Remember it every day = watch it grow.

Let go of your thought = have faith.

Until you bring the harvest home.

Follow The Love.

Let go of anger, let go of fear, let go of all unloving thoughts.

Follow your dreams, your dreams create our world.

May our minds all work together in the flow of Love.

Share The Love

Send love to each other every day.

Remember to honor your friends every time you see them.

And know their Love is a special gift.

Make A Heart Print!

The Heart Prints that we make on each other,

will reflect each others thoughts like a mirror.

Look in the mirror and see me.

You And I, Are One!

The memorable times we've had together

are the tiniest most simplest moments

that allow our souls to connect.

We are connected at our heart strings.

Can You Choose Love?

Even in the hardest times?

By the thoughts you think you create Love or Fear things.

You get to choose in any situation.

Be Thankful For Life, It's A Present!

Keep your life in balance and take time for fun,

time for your body, and time for your love for each other.

Trust In Your Heart

Your heart will lead you to your **G**reatest **O**f **D**esires.

That will be the path that you

will create, by the choices that you make in any situation.

Most Important!

Take time to know, *The Spirit Within You.*

There is a Spirit within you that needs to be awakened!

Then you will be in harmony with all of Life.

You are part of a family of Love.

This is your world

We must take care of it.

Remember, when I see you and you see me, I turn the ME into WE just look in the mirror, because you and I are one.

www.ingramcontent.com/pod-product-compliance
Lightning Source LLC
Chambersburg PA
CBHW061148010526
44118CB00026B/2915